John Boorman's
NATURE
DIARY
One Eye, One Finger

John Boorman's
NATURE DIARY

One Eye, One Finger

With illustrations by
SUSAN MORLEY

THE LILLIPUT PRESS
DUBLIN

First published 2020 by
THE LILLIPUT PRESS
62–63 Arbour Hill
Dublin 7, Ireland
www.lilliputpress.ie

A CIP record for this publication is available from The British Library.

10 9 8 7 6 5 4 3 2 1

HB ISBN 978 1 84351 795 5
PB ISBN 978 1 84351 806 8

The Lilliput Press gratefully acknowledges the financial support
of the Arts Council /An Chomhairle Ealaíon.

Set in 11pt on 15pt Adobe Garamond Pro by Niall McCormack.
Printed in Poland by Drukarnia Skleniarz.

CONTENTS

'April is the cruellest month'
–T.S. Eliot

PREFACE

In the glorious summer of 1969 I was doing the post-production of my film *Leo the Last* at Ardmore Studios.

We explored the glens and lochs of the Wicklow mountains. Would it not be good to find a cottage to come back to for holidays? We were living in LA. One day we were shown this rather grim old Protestant vicarage and its land. A river ran through it, and there were many fine oaks. It was being auctioned the following day. There was no time to have it surveyed. I put it out of my mind.

I happened to be in Dublin the next day. I was passing James Adam's, the auctioneers, and there was a picture of the house in the window. I wandered in out of curiosity. The auction had already begun.

I had a strange, out-of-body experience. I was hovering on the high, ornate ceiling, looking down at the auction. Two people were bidding for it, and one of them appeared to be me. Suddenly I was down among the mortals, being congratulated. I had bought a house. What was I going to tell Christel, my wife?

My subconscious had made the decision for me. We were to live in Ireland.

Christel bravely took on the house and transformed it into a magical place. Our four children happily grew up there, running wild. I was glad they were not growing up in LA; nor did I want to go back to England, with its absurd monarchy and pernicious class system.

The four children grew up and went out into the world.

Many years later, a second wife, three more children. I made movies around the world, but always brought them back to Ardmore to edit.

Lee was nine and Lili Mae six when Isabella left the marriage, taking the children with her. I took them out to dinner once a week, and they came up for the odd weekend, but it is fifteen years since they lived here, so I was delighted when they decided to isolate with me for the duration of the lockdown.

A curious fox cub, still with tufts of white fur, took to peering into the kitchen while I was having my breakfast and it occurred to me that with scant human activity and silent roads and skies, the wildlife might venture out. I decided to keep a diary of my observations. My neighbour, Kathy Gilfillan, read my April diary and urged me to continue and to publish it. Now the dynamic changed. I was writing for others, not only for myself. I went out each day and reported on what I saw.

1 APRIL

A heavy cloud cover and stillness

As I step out of the conservatory facing north, supported by my pusher, the first thing that catches my eye is the dying sycamore, which escapes death every year by producing a healthy crop of leaves. Surely it can't pull that trick yet again? It looks so decrepit. Then I see the boulder with Celtic spirals carved into it by my friend Brother Anthony, a Benedictine monk. The oak I planted at its side has its branches flung out wide as though calling for help. I am hoping that in time the tree's roots will clasp the rock.

To the right of the rock is a tall Scots pine with a scary swing hanging from a high branch. A mile behind it is the steep, round hill that announces Annamoe as you come from Roundwood. A little further to the right rise the perfect, fan-shaped upper branches of our most majestic Great Oak.

I go down the driveway. The house is on my right, and a little further down is an enormous, rather pushy, eight-stemmed sycamore. It competes for airspace with a cluster of four Californian redwoods, the tallest trees we have by far, but I have a sparse relationship with them. They stick together, darkly aloof. Dr Sam Synge, brother of the poet, was the vicar here in the 1920s and probably planted them, just a hundred years ago. Too close to the redwoods on one side and too close to the house on the other, I am always threatening to cut down the sycamore, but in response it puts on such a dazzling display of leaves that I am obliged to recant.

I pass under the four limes and their twiggy bottoms that straddle the driveway and then a great curve of the river opens up. On the other side of the water are the many groves of trees we planted that take the eye to the humpback bridge, which marks our boundary.

The driveway passes under the birch arch, very patchy at present. On a slope, way over to the left, is a range of ancient oaks that are so majestic I want to genuflect.

OAKS ON SLOPES

Old oaks are mostly found on slopes.
For on any land fit to grow or graze,
The oak is felled and fashioned into boats,
Or floorboards or to keep the fire ablaze.
Once the master of all the land,
It now clings to slopes as best it can.

On the left of the range of oaks is that magnificent Great Oak with its fan-shaped upper branches we admired above. It is 70 yards away and I regret that I cannot cross the rough ground on my pusher to examine it closer.

To the right, hanging over the driveway, are aspens, more oaks, hazel bushes, a vast, shapeless, overgrown larch, and finally my beloved twin oak, which hangs precariously over the river. I sit on the bench under the twin oak and watch the river go by.

This is my minute–vast universe, the only walk on which my legs will carry me.

The winter hangs grimly on

Nothing moving except for the horse chestnut, which has quietly produced a crop of big, dark green, shiny leaves. His are always first out and first to drop. I hope there will be conkers this year. The chestnut stands next to my only beech, side by side like suspects in an identity parade: the O P W [Office of Public Works] had a policy to eradicate them from public places on the grounds that they are not indigenous, only naturalized, like me. There was such an outcry against these beautiful trees being slaughtered that the O P W were forced to abandon it. I suspect the case against the beech is that it served as an avenue up to the grand houses of the gentry. I have a wonderful painting of a beech by Susan Morley.

Signs of spring

Tiny flowers have popped up round the base of the oaks – a fanfare to wake them from their winter sleep? Some buttercups have ventured out, just an advance squad to report back. The badger had dug a hole near the twin oak, looking for worms, I imagine, and frustrating, I should think, since the hole was deep. What it revealed were dozens of white pods waiting to jump out. They weren't around a few days ago. Grasses, I expect.

We have a pair of lover birches clasped in a silver embrace. Moving slowly, I notice things I used to flash past.

Colder today and the brave ones are running for cover

Those couple of warm days have woken the red squirrels and they are ravenously eating the twin oak's acorns from last year. The squirrels have been there for the fifty years of my stay, several generations, I suppose. We had an invasion of greys. I set a trap with peanut butter. The greedy greys would not allow the reds anywhere near the peanut butter, so the greys perished.

One acorn from the twin oak evaded the squirrels, the mice, the badger and the deer and self-planted. As it grew, the deer ate off its crown. It sent out a branch as a lopsided leader and celebrated with a growth of healthy leaves. It lives under its mother's wing and begins to flourish. Nature's way – if you make a hundred thousand acorns, one might stick. A few million people will come up with an Einstein or a Beatle.

The pandemic has brought so much death, but also a soothing silence.

East wind gusts

I have written of my anxiety about my twin oak, which leans out over the river in its quest for morning light. The light of the rest of the day is hidden by other trees. This huge weight is held by straining roots. When I examine the tree closely I see it has dropped two large boughs on the riverside, reducing the weight by a lot. Which part of the oak makes that decision? Is it the straining roots? Or the intelligent fungus that steers this monolith?

A bunch of primroses has appeared, tucked under the lee of the twin oak. We are two weeks behind the spring at sea level. The east wind gusts are like playful punches but they threaten to tip me over, me and my pusher.

Warm, strong wind and sunshine, exhilarating after the still, grey days just passed. Lili and Lee and I sat on the bench next to the twin oak and watched the river flow past and they fell into the same seductive reverie that I always experience.

The violent wind has dropped, leaving a peaceful stillness

The only sound is the river, no longer raging, just gurgling.

I count five bird songs (not including the boring wood pigeon with its broken call). I can't fit the song to the bird, with the exception of the blackbird and the song thrush, neither of which nest here. Mine seem to be little birds with high-pitched calls like boy sopranos. The resting trees and the deep stillness strangely fill me. How much it took to do that – of space or time or both?

I sent Gerry to the orchard to prune the fruit trees this morning, in the nick of time. They are only three years planted and need attention. Gerry shares our isolation and works four days a week and does a lot of stuff I used to do myself. I prolong my life through others. The corona virus has gifted us silent skies, clear water in Venice and reduced emissions. All governments are wedded to growth, the very thing we cannot afford. The virus has done for climate change what governments should have been doing – but great sacrifices are needed at a terrible cost to avert the end of life on earth.

Is the virus less vindictive to poorer countries? I dread the consequences of trying to inflict a shutdown on India.

A sunny morning and warmer. Wind still from the SE

The low sun lights up the silver birch. It flashes at me as I make my slow progress down the drive. Overnight, wild garlic has appeared at the foot of the limes, announcing itself with that heady scent. The symbiotic moss is thick and luminous on my beloved twin oak. It rises 8 ft up the bark, a warm blanket against the prevailing wind. I sit quietly on the bench, thinking.

Poor Boris Johnson is in intensive care. *Be careful what you wish for.* He wanted it so much: weekends at Chequers, servants and power. All political careers end in failure, it is said. The virus strikes high and low. Leo Varadker, the Irish taoiseach, goes back to doing some doctoring, but only on the phone, and only on Tuesdays.

THE VIRUS

It stopped the clocks,
Locked us up,
Banned cars from the roads,
Shot down all the planes,
Played havoc with the Stock Exchange,
Taught us to wash our hands,
Four times every day,
Its iron grip on life and death,
Takes our breath away.

A heavy blanket of cloud this morning

Thirty years ago we planted a Japanese garden on the slope above the house. There is a tea house where I often used to sit and think. While I was thinking, the bamboo spread like a virus and strangled more tender plants, the flowering shrubs and delicate flowers. The battle has continued. When my daughter Telsche died, we planted, in her name, a Himalayan larch. The bamboo has surrounded it, and we have fought to keep it free. The larch is tall and slender and has parchment-like bark. I can peel it off and write upon it. I had plans to write greetings to her friends, but never got round to it. Now I can barely climb the slope. In fact, I can't.

The sun has punched a hole in the cloud cover. I will venture out and see what is moving. The incongruously big blossoms on the azaleas and rhododendrons are flaunting themselves. They are here and gone in a couple of weeks and we endure their ugly bushes for the rest of the year.

That SE wind is now a light breeze, mostly fading away altogether. Nothing much stirring. The monkey puzzle looks exotically alien in this drab winter landscape. The river is low. No rain for three weeks. It was incessant in February and early March. The rain clattered down the Sally Gap mountain to Luggala where my dear friend, the very late Garech Browne, held court and surveyed Loch Tay, which in turn flows down to Loch Dan where the little Avonmore river has to carry that entire deluge.

FOR GARECH

Rain hammers onto granite rock,
Bounces into furious mist,
Races down the mountainside,
Roaring and white at Luggala,
Where Garech dispenses noblesse oblige,
To pipers and poets all under siege.

Sublime music keeps the storm at bay,
The deluge swerves past the house,
Wall of water judders the Sepulchre,
A brother and sister tremble below,
Loch Tay swallows the angry rain,
Into its magic glacial depths.

Merlin conjured Excalibur from here,
To serve a telling of the myth.
Swollen, bursting Loch Tay,
Disgorges the riotous water,
To a rocky stretch of river,
That puts manners on it, slows it.

Turns up tamed at Loch Dan,
Gently cradled by soft hills,
Its shallow shingle sought by salmon,
To lay their eggs and die all spent.
The Avonmore river drains it all,
Two lakes and a mountainside.

The weight of water runs for the sea,
But not before passing me.
I stand at my swimming hole,
As the river hurtles past.
'Come with me,' the river calls,
'Come with me to the sea.'
A perfect way to go, but courage fails.

On summer days I stand on its bank,
Naked, waiting to be invited in,
Unworthy, the river will not have me.
On days when I am granted entry,
I swim across to the Rock of Truth,
Embraced, washed clean of sin,
The wanted, wordless benediction.

9 APRIL

A proper warm spring day

Sun burst through the bedroom window, saying *Come on out.*

The twiggy base of the limes is crowded with buds, and the tops of the birches are flying into leaf. Even the careful old oaks are showing a kind of yellow pre-leaf. Someone fired the starter gun and the race is on. The low, sluggish river of yesterday is running for its life. It must have rained heavily in the mountains, but not a drop down here. The grass is suddenly luminous.

I didn't get out till ten. I feel I somehow missed the moment.

10 APRIL

Hazy sun this morning

Warm and still, soporific. Lee and I wander down, the excitement of yesterday's rite of spring nowhere to be seen. Buds quietly becoming leaves. Bees buzzing.

Lee spotted the kingfisher this morning during his morning swim. It is some years since I saw the bird flash past, skimming the river's surface, my diminishing eyesight not up to it. The other fisher of this stretch of river I can see clearly: the heron stands stock-still on a rock in the river, its wings folded tightly, pretending to be a stick. When he takes flight he opens his 5 ft wingspan and soars up into the sky.

The huge overgrown larch, sporting its new crop of needles, saying to them, 'Give me more carbon, I intend to grow even bigger.'

Trees have viruses too. Dutch elm disease wiped out a whole species and changed the landscape of England. In the rainforests of Brazil, a particular species of trees in the path of the virus develop antibodies to stop it. No one knows how the afflicted trees can somehow warn their fellows of what's to come.

Last year my neighbour, Declan Murphy, found a rare great spotted woodpecker nesting about a mile downstream. Its location was a closely guarded secret. Declan watched all year and wrote a fine book about it. Now we have a woodpecker tapping away at one of our oaks. The sharp, percussive noise seems to silence the other birds, or bring them to attention. I wonder if it is the same woodpecker?

It is Good Friday. Jesus saying 'Why hast thou forsaken me?' could so easily have been the abrupt end to Christianity. A clever Hindko scholar asked me to explain. 'First you crucify your God, then you eat him every Sunday. Why?'

11 APRIL

Warm and still

Boris is released from intensive care, but can't function for a month. His dreary cabinet of Brexiteers have been revealed as a third-rate bunch as they try to fill his tap-dancing shoes. A lacerating attack on Boris by Fintan O'Toole in *The Irish Times* that no British journalist would dare to write when the man has just been snatched from the jaws of death.

Which reminds me of the two thorn bushes on the drive. *Why don't you cut those ugly things down?* I am regularly urged. But they have always been there. I would miss them. They are coming into their modest leaf, a small, dull affair. What are their fierce prickles defending – their berries from birds? A bird has been singing in the second bush. My old gardener, Jim, used to say, 'The devil needs somewhere to perch. You don't want him coming into the house.'

12 APRIL

Rain

Easter Sunday. Lee is busy with the lamb and Lili Mae is making rhubarb crumble. In a godless world the food symbols remain, divorced from their religious origins. As I prepare to go out I am forced back by rain, the first for three or four weeks. We can do with it. Perhaps it will urge spring along.

How lucky we are to be here with all this space. I think of urban flat-dwellers. It must be so hard. This virus raises so many questions about how we live and work. It will be a different world.

13 APRIL

Sunshine, but a bitter cold NE wind

Easter Monday. As the death toll soars, mounting criticism of a floundering government in Britain.

I go out and brave the wind. Thousands of little yellow bud covers, ejected by the emerging birch leaves, litter the tarmac below. The birch arch is gradually restoring itself as the leaves reach out from both sides and will soon become an arch again.

For fifty years no pesticide has touched this land, yet our insect life is sparse. There are a few dragonflies down at the swimming hole, and some common butterflies. I haven't seen a ladybird in years. The midges used to drive us crazy – you could not go out on a summer's evening without being eaten alive. The harsh winter two years ago killed them off and they have not been back. We have bees and wasps and houseflies, but no ants. We used to have hedgehogs, but no longer. I have two meadows I am rewilding. Am I doing something wrong? Is it too late?

14 APRIL

Frost this morning, but the sun is shining out of a blue sky

Thinking about missing animals: there used to be frogs and toads, but no more. The pond by the kitchen was always glutinous with their spawn at this time of year. We never had moles, the delightful hero of *Wind in the Willows* that would push up a pile of soil on suburban lawns in England.

Lee corrects me on the frogs. At the far end of our land is an acre of swampy land, which, he says, is heaving with frogs. Good news. He also tells me about his morning swim – crackling frost underfoot, vapour rising from the river turned to fog by the backlit sun: magical and painful.

I walk out a little later. The air is cold but there is no wind and the sun rules. By the river, on the bank, grasses have sprouted, such lovely variety. They are cropped and mown and keep coming back for more. We live on their cousins; wheat and barley and corn and rice (I think rice is a grass). Lili picked a bunch of clover flowers and they hold their place on the kitchen table next to the orchid. Grass needs water and we have had so little rain.

Another sunny day

We are halfway through the month. Still locked down.

The Avonmore river comes down from Loch Tay to Loch Dan. Both lochs are pure and unpolluted. It was an especial joy, when bathing in Loch Tay, to drink as you swam. Loch Dan is equally pure. The Avonmore, which drains them, passes through agricultural land until it reaches Annamoe bridge. The inhabitants traditionally threw their rubbish over the bridge into the river: this was corrected, but some still do so at night. Tourists throw stuff out of car windows as they go over the bridge. The other day when the river was low, Lee waded down the length of our stretch and filled two large black bags with beer cans, bottles and the ubiquitous plastic bags. With no tourists to blame, let's see what happens.

A warm, still, sunny day

A rare, precious day when we forgive Ireland for all its miserable weather. (Lee: 'Dad, I love the Irish weather and so do you.')

Down by the twin oak, I fall into a timeless reverie. Two birds singing in a deeper register, another with a rasping cry – bigger birds, I feel. No swallows yet. Garech used to winter in India and we would say of him that he came back with the swallows.

Lee and his black Alsatian came looking for me, concerned. 'Did you fall asleep, Dad?' He made us nettle soup with wild garlic. Delicious.

The leaves are gradually opening up. They are the workers, taking carbon dioxide from the air and by photosynthesis giving carbon to the tree and sending oxygen back into the air. In the autumn the tree withdraws the valuable nitrogen from the leaf, then casts it off, kills it. The leaf is a pliant slave and we rejoice in its unconscious beauty.

Another sunny morning

An east wind and rain promised later, much needed.

I sit on the bench by the twin oak. I feel rather sheepish, having accused it of killing its leaves. The birds are busy mating and nesting, obeying the same instincts that drive us to have and raise children. Our subconscious is calling all the shots. We have to accept this with good grace; that we are not in charge. It does all my best writing and has all my best film ideas. I shamefully accept the credit. Does the subconscious control the plant world as well as ours? Is the subconscious the underlying force that impels and regulates all of nature, including ours?

The wind is half-hearted. It blows a gust, then peters out. A few puffy clouds, but none carrying rain. The rain comes through in the afternoon. I go out and let it fall on my face.

18 APRIL

Cloud and rain

Saturday. Lee is sleeping in. All week he works on the computer doing the long hours of legal drudgery that a young lawyer must endure for a couple of years before he is let loose on clients.

There is a heavy blanket of cloud out there. I have breakfast with Lili. She seems melancholic, sad even, which pains me. We are all three locked down here.

A misty rain out there, Lee tells me.

I go down the hill from the house. The trees look mournful, their heads in the clouds. I turn back, a loss of power. I regret the half bottle of white wine I had with the chicken last night. I toil back up the hill. I get back drenched in clammy sweat. Sleep in my chair. Wake up cold. Lili serves some reviving soup. I allow the natural world to get along without me.

Moist and misty and still

Lee's muscular power and speed over the ground are in such contrast to my slow passage and dimming eyes that I have come to depend on his observations, but this journal must, at heart, be the about an old man's connections with the natural world. At the highest level are the occasional strong connections I feel with trees. I experience a discernible energy coming from them that is soothing and enveloping. I try to respond. It is non-verbal. Trees give off endorphins, which make us feel calm when we walk through a wood, but this is of a different order.

A greyness. No planes, no traffic, no wind playing with the trees. Only the assertive yellow of the gorse flowers. They are always there ('When gorse is out of bloom, kissing is out of season') but are especially vibrant in spring, reminding farmers that, despite all their efforts, gorse lives on.

Feeling much stronger than yesterday, I go down to the twin oak to watch the river. My role is to respect the silence. I sit quietly. A deep peace envelops me, then I start to feel transparent. I have no substance. I am melting away into the soil. Is this a death? I sit up with a jerk and head for home. The sycamore is vigorously leafing. I pass the Japanese garden. I see it is exploding with blossom, in defiance of the perfect greyness of the day. They wave to me as I pass: purple, deep red, white with a yellow centre.

I wonder if Lili has made lunch.

20 APRIL

Sunny morning but a sharp east wind

Oddly the twiggy bottoms on the limes come into leaf well before the rest of the tree. Most trees leaf first at the top, the ones with most access to the sun. The lime is original in many ways. It starts leafing at the bottom and works its way up. In July it bursts into blossom.

The tops of the birches are just touching their sisters on the other side, but it is not yet an arch. The hazel bushes have sprung into leaf. We cut them back during the winter, but two of them are still masking the perfect Great Oak. The hazel has an ambition to be a tree but I have often to remind it that it is a bush, and cut it down to size.

No sign of leaves from the oaks or the aspens.

Hardly any birdsong this morning, nearly a total silence. Is there a hawk about? The wind has veered to the north.

A clear blue sky but a cold NE wind

The eight-stemmed sycamore is bursting with its big bright green leaves, determined to wipe out the redwoods. A little farther down the drive and I am among the limes, observing the progression of their leafing: the twiggy bottoms first and then gradually working its way upward. Still no sign of life from the oaks. More birch twigs touching, not quite an arch yet, but soon.

Started out grey, but the sun showing fitfully

At 10.30 am I venture out. Lee tells me that yesterday the river was warm for the first time this season.

I hear that ladybirds and daisies are seen all over the west of Ireland. Our altitude always costs us a couple of degrees and a couple of weeks.

A cold north wind, the sun giving up. It felt dead out there. Only two birds calling plus the mournful wood pigeon.

Why is there such heavy moss on the twin oak and not on other oaks? Could it be because the twin oak leans, so it is less vertical and therefore easier to climb? Or is it because that side is mostly shady? A bit of both? Does the oak welcome the moss or resent it?

We know the oak is sensitive to its bark. There is a bacterium that is a nitrogen-fixer. When it attaches itself to the bark, the oak feeds it carbohydrates to persuade it to stay. I always stroke the bark as a greeting whenever I visit the twin oak, which is most days.

I am writing this in the afternoon. The clouds have dispersed and we have yet another bright blue sky.

I am clearing the view of my perfectly shaped Great Oak by cutting back the hazel bushes that obscure it. There is a birch that intrudes. Lee pleads for its life. I have agreed to inspect it with him tomorrow.

The warmest day yet

Another sunny morning inviting me out. Still no daisies, but plenty of dandelion flowers.

As I wait for the reluctant oaks to leaf I ponder and wonder how the oak came to dominate northern Europe after the last Ice Age. As the ice receded we are told that the birch led the charge north, followed by the oaks. How the oaks became so dominant is hard to understand. It is fragile when young and so succulent to animals. Lee reminds me that wolves were hunting the deer, which didn't give them the leisure to nibble saplings. We could do with some wolves here. We are overrun by deer.

The Hamilton wood, which leads down to Loch Dan, is primeval. I have walked it and fallen under its spell over and over. I filmed *Lancelot* there, he riding through a carpet of bluebells and Merlin instructing the young Arthur as he gets tangled in the wood.

As the ancient trees fell, there were no young trees to replace them and the gaps in the canopy led to an invasion of weeds. I told Caroline Hamilton, who owns the wood, that it was dying. The deer ate all the young oak shoots. She put up a high deer fence around its perimeter about five years ago and it is finally reviving.

The mystery of the oak persists and we feel it our duty to protect it. If there were no more oaks, it would be all over.

Calm and warm

Yet another sunny morning, but by ten it has clouded over. A lot of tiny blue wood anemones have appeared, but still no daisies. The river is low, no rain.

When an oak is fully grown it continues to put out leaves and collect carbon. Some of it goes to replace lost twigs, but what happens to the surplus? A 300-year-old oak has lost most of its branches, it looks barely alive. Does it continue to put out leaves?

My narrow world opened up magically this afternoon when Lee brought me in the wheelchair to the huge, perfect Great Oak I have been admiring from afar for fifty years. I had asked Gerry to cut down a small tree that was partially obscuring the magnificence of the Great Oak. Both trees stand on a steep slope, too steep for the wheelchair. Lee carried me up in his arms and I was able to lean against the Great Oak's massive girth and give thanks. I had to wipe a tear from my eye to view it properly. I was in awe.

Lee and I then examined the small tree in contention. Although it was only 9 ft tall, its bark suggested a much older tree, stunted by proximity to such a goliath. It was snarled up with ivy. It was showing some leaves at its top. Lee thought they were oak leaves, but I pointed out that none of the oaks had leafed yet. It was a stunted thorn. We agreed to strip off all the ivy and then take another look.

Lee wheeled me down to the river and we followed its course to the spot where he had transplanted the four young ash saplings. Two of them had perished, their smooth grey bark stripped by deer. The other two had survived and flourished, the only ash we have on the place.

He then wheeled me into the walled garden where he spotted a single daisy and a yellow pansy growing next to it. All the fruit trees were showing healthy blossoms.

We came back to the house and I sat down to write this.

25 APRIL

Cloud cover, but no wind and quite warm

I am still under the spell of finally meeting the Great Oak. I can tell if an oak is aware of me. Here he felt distant, remote, but harmonious.

I walk down to the twin oak. On the way I run into a group of daisies – at last! Things are changing. Three new bird songs and all sound exited. The sun tries to break through the cloud cover.

In the foreground are the branches of the twin oak. They are leafing! The leaves were unfolding before my eyes. Beneath, the river dawdled past, unaware of the momentous events unfolding above. I searched the other oaks to see if they were leafing, but they were too high to tell.

I walk home to bring the news.

Sunny early on then overcast with misty rain

I woke up early, drawn to the open window by a cacophony of shrill noise – the dawn chorus. The density and range was astonishing, then it petered out and we were left with individual birdcalls.

I walked down the hill from the house. The eight-stemmed sycamore's big, bright leaves were screaming at me, *Look at us*, and I have to say they looked pretty good.

I was glad to see the limes leafing their way up their trees.

A bird singing in each of the gorse bushes. The birds are low to the ground but protected by the prickles – a haven. Now I have a better excuse for not cutting them down.

The birch arch is still not complete, the ceiling a little patchy. The aspens are not leafing yet. The Great Oak is showing leaf, as are all the oaks to some degree. Its filigree pattern of branches will soon be obscured by a covering of leaves. A few more daisies have popped up, a bouquet to congratulate the oaks – like me, they feared they never would. In these bad times anything is possible, but we can at least celebrate renewal.

Grey skies and a cold east wind

Lee snared a rabbit and it got its revenge. We ate it last night. It was tough as old boots.

The lime trees' leaves are still working their way up the trees. The wild garlic at the base of their trunks now in flower. The hazel bushes still partially masking the Great Oak. Must get Gerry to do a little more shaving.

The birch arch still has a bald patch.

The leaves on the twin oak slowly emerging into a cold grey day. Not much to report after the momentous events of the last days.

28 APRIL

Early morning sun, but welcome rain forecast later

The wind is still in the N E, bringing cold air. We haven't had the prevailing wind from the S W that ushers in rain from the Atlantic. I will hurry out to make my observations. With three days to go till the end of the month, it seems that spring will have just about sprung before May Day.

Grey skies

A light rain falling, not enough to slake the thirst of the bone-dry earth.

11 am. The rain has stopped. I venture out.

I hear a plane passing overhead. The first for a very long time. In another world.

The birch arch has finally closed its top and it darkens a little as you go under it. It is dripping slightly.

I was pleased to see the aspens budding.

SW prevailing wind

Happily, it rained heavily overnight. Cold and a bright sun this morning.

On this, the last day of the month, I step out, as I did on the first, from the conservatory. On the left stand my two suspects, the chestnut and the beech, rejoicing in their rich covering of leaves. A little to the right, our half-dead sycamore is flouting yet another death-defying cover of healthy leaves. Further down is the chiselled boulder. The oak I planted next to it has yet to leaf, but the white beam next to it is in full bloom, its white under-leaf glowing with light.

Then we see the hill, a mile away, with the naughty gorse crawling up it. Much closer is the reliable Scots pine that gives us greenery through the winter. A little further over, the Great Oak offers a display of its fan of upper leaves.

As I venture further down the drive I see a corner of the Japanese garden, blooms still flashing colour at me.

The redwoods soar into the heavens, darkly dominant. The ambitious eight-stem sycamore is intent on blocking out the redwoods. It gets crowded down there; we are soon on top of the four limes, just about managing to leaf the tops of their trees.

I come upon the two gorse bushes, looking less hostile now with their leaves hiding their prickles.

On my right is the monkey puzzle to remind us what trees looked like to the dinosaurs, and behind it, the great arc of the river. Further down are the aspens – they started tentative budding yesterday and are coming on apace. I look forward to their fluttering leaves.

On my left is the magnificent Great Oak, now released from the embrace of the hazel bushes. Further along the slope is the line of forty-five oaks, a majestic chorus to the Great Oak's singular perfection.

Hanging over the drive is the enormous overgrown larch.

Finally, I reach my beloved twin oak. I touch its bark to announce my presence and sit on the bench. The tree's lower branches dip into the river, causing tiny eddies and making their leaves flutter. I sense the tree casting its spell. I fall willingly under it.

The end of April 2020.

1 MAY

Sunny

Whatever force regulates the rhythm of trees must have a calendar handy because the tentative budding of yesterday becomes the rich leaves of today, the first of May.

2 MAY

Another warm, sunny day

The slightly vulgar chestnut is suddenly displaying a great show of candles, offering a birthday party for summer.

3 MAY

A cloudy start

The sun soon chases the clouds away. A chilly S E wind.

The air is so rich that I stagger around, drunk on the wonder of spring exploding before my eyes like fireworks.

4 MAY

Sunny

That s e wind, however, keeps us on our toes.

I sober up and pay attention to what is happening around me. The Great Oak is pumping in excess of a hundred gallons of water per day up the great height of the tree; no one knows how. It stores water in its trunk and on the surfaces of its roots. The taproot goes down to the water table and sucks up more. The twin oak, being close to the river, has an ample supply.

Broken cloud

The central mystery of the tree is how that water gets up there. I was taught it was by capillary action, that the surface tension of water dragged it up. Even as a schoolboy that explanation felt shaky. When I railed against it, I was told by the priest that God moved in mysterious ways. More persuasive was the theory that as the leaf's moisture evaporated it caused a tiny vacuum that, multiplied by a hundred thousand leaves, becomes a great force. Plausible, but the water rises most vigorously before the leaves bud – *vide* maple syrup.

Fluffy clouds about, but no rain expected

If God created the world, He found that everything worked except getting water to go up a tree, so He decided to make water vapour lighter than air (what a cheat) so that it would float up to form clouds and expand when it turns to ice instead of contracting like everything else. But when it came to getting it 300 ft up a tree ... solve this and find God.

H_2O is neutral since the hydrogen ion has a positive charge of +1 and oxygen has a negative charge of -2, but when water finds itself against certain surfaces, it can take on another hydrogen ion, becoming H_3O^+, with a positive charge of +1. Now we are talking electricity, which no one really understands. However, we know what it can do. Pumping water up a tree – no problem. Just another theory.

Blue skies and sunshine

We are told that the birds have learnt to sing louder to be heard over the traffic din. They should pipe down a bit, now they are the only sounds that break the new silence. The swallows are back, flying high, feeding on spiders that travel on high winds with their webs extended.

Often we wake up to find a hundred cobwebs in the garden. Where do they come from?

8 MAY

Another warm, sunny day

Lee urges me to go with him to our swimming hole. It is a trek. At the far end of our stretch of river, only 300 yards, but hard enough over grass with my pusher.

Last summer I ventured into the river alone, after an absence of several years. My feet and lower legs were leaden. I found I could not raise them. I lacked flotation. In order to swim you need to be horizontal, or halfway so. I was vertical. I tried to paddle with my arms to shallower water, but made little progress. I was being pulled under. I paddled hard with my arms, but could not regain the surface. Not a bad way to go, in my favourite place in the world. I could no longer hold my breath. I let it out, involuntarily. I sucked in water exactly as my feet touched the bottom of shallower water. The feet that betrayed me now saved me, as I rose above the surface, gasping for air. I spewed up the water I had sucked up into my stomach (the lungs shut down).

Old age is a series of retreats, and it seemed that swimming was another.

So today I arrived nervous and exhausted to the swimming hole. I slumped onto the bench that faces the river and the diving board from which I used to enter the water.

Lee and I stand naked, facing the river. The sun has shone all day and there is no wind. The trees that line the river are perfectly reflected in the still water: birch, ash and alder. A few yards further down, the river runs over shallow shingle and the sun sets it on dazzling fire, calm and frenzy, side by side.

Lee helps me in. I have a buoyancy device strapped to my chest. I am a nervous child, learning to swim. Where is the long-distance swimmer of once? I swim across to the Rock of Truth, Lee as an escort. We swim and swim. I am reborn. I rejoice. Thank you, Lee.

Biting NE wind and bitterly cold

I venture out, but am driven back by squally showers. The contrast with yesterday is extreme. The light in Ireland is beautiful but treacherous, no continuity. It rained every day on the long shoot of *Excalibur*. We waited and waited for those moments of magic light.

10 MAY

Still that cold NE wind

Gerry tells me there was a frost in some places. The wind is giving the tender young leaves a violent shaking. Whatever force directs the changes of tree cycles has no influence on weather, which is entirely unruly.

11 MAY

Sunny, but bitterly cold.

I wrap up and set out. Lili calls me back. 'I thought you were doing this for fun. Come back and have another cup of coffee.'

Sunny, but clouding over

No wind. Warmth seems to rise from the earth. The sun waves now and then.

I start down from the house. I see that the eight-stemmed sycamore has plastered its leaves all over the redwoods and is largely blocking them out, but the leading redwood rises 10 ft above the sycamore like a cathedral spire.

The thick redwood needles rattle if you brush them as you pass, coarse and leathery. They are fire-resistant. *We need protection. We might be around for a thousand years.* The 300-year-old oaks are like children compared to them.

Clusters of bluebells appear at the bottom of the trees. Garech had a huge carpet at Luggala, but it disappeared twenty years ago, eaten by deer. I love the blue haze that hangs over bluebell carpets; it is almost narcotic.

My neighbour Lainey, the Queen of Cashmere, has gifted me an electric Zimmer no longer used by her mother. It will allow me to probe a little more of the demesne.

Bright sun, icy wind

I set out early, encouraged by a bright sun making sharp shadows.

As I step outside, I am stunned by the glory of the rich-leaved trees. There is a strong, icy NE wind and I hurry back for my coat. I see there is cloud about.

A bird sings in the first thorn bush. If, for whatever reason, a bird needs to sing low to the earth, a thorn bush is the only safe place it can go, the prickles protecting it from marauding cats. A good enough reason not to cut down thorn bushes. There was also the belief that the thorns protected it from lightning.

> Beware of an oak,
> it draws the stroke;
> avoid an ash,
> it counts the flash;
> creep under the thorn,
> it can save you from harm.

A little further down on the left, the Great Oak is head and shoulders above the other oaks, its majesty threatened only by the hazels masking parts of it like badly applied green wallpaper. When it rains heavily, the grass in front of the Great Oak becomes a pond.

Trees reflected in a pond
Abandon their stern solidity.
They ripple and prance,
Twigs touch and flirt,
Their lives enhanced
By this liquid dance.
But be constantly alert,
A trunk with a swaying skirt,
Its dignity can be slightly hurt.

The ancients thought the hazel was the tree of knowledge and its nuts the givers of wisdom. What they do here is mask the majesty of the oaks and feed the squirrels nuts in September.

We come to the vast overgrown larch, its branches heavy with new, bright green needles, weighing its limbs down to the ground all around the tree, looking as though it is curtsying to the Great Oak.

Finally, I reach the twin oak and sit on the bench. The river runs softly. I wonder again, is it a single force that brings the swallows back, that urges the trees to leaf, that sets the birds singing for a mate? Is it the same subconscious that presses us to have and raise children, that helps us to write our books and guides the paintbrush? We learn that more of our impulses and decisions are taken not by our conscious minds but by the unconscious.

There was a quick refreshing shower of rain – now the sun prevails and the wind bites.

A frosty morning

It was five degrees below last night. Clearly the weather is not connected to the force I wrote of before, it goes its own wild way.

Sunny with a few little puffy clouds that the sun bullies out of its sight. Same chilly N E wind.

In Wicklow we have way too many wild deer. They are accused of infecting cattle with T B. They eat everything, including young tree bark and all the oak saplings. Consequently, the oak woods are dying. When we come across a noble stag standing in a wood, we can convince ourselves we are out in the wild, but where are the wolves when we need them?

Our cattle graze all day, happily un-hunted. Cows would be extinct if we didn't eat them.

MAMMALS 1

All mammals do is eat and fornicate.
Sheep and cows graze all day long,
Crop the grass and masticate,
Will only pause to procreate,
And end their days on someone's plate.

We mammals are busy between meals,
Warring and whoring and making deals,
Painting pictures, writing songs,
Devising laws, righting wrongs,
Asking God, saying prayers,
Lying, cheating, having affairs,
All to convince us of the lie,
That none of us is going to die.

Despite the cold night, a few brave wood anemones have put their heads above the parapets. Their lovely blue colour surely relates them to the bluebell.

Overcast and still

As I arrived in the kitchen for breakfast there was an urgent tapping on the window. It was a blackbird with glossy black feathers and it was tapping with its bright yellow beak, staring at me with beady eyes. After a few seconds it flew off. I can't recall seeing a blackbird on our land. I went outside and looked for it and listened for its song, one of the few I can recognize, but it had vanished.

The sky was heavily overcast, darkening the day. There was no wind. The silence was palpable, only fractured by the little birds tweeting in a high register as though the silence had swallowed up anything deeper.

I walked down. Blackberry plants are tangled up with the thorn bushes and they are in flower. I look forward to eating them in September if I live that long. At my age I take no long-term engagements.

There are hundreds of little white flowers dancing around the feet of the oaks. They have five double petals – stitchwort, sometimes called shirt buttons; my mother called them wedding cakes. Exquisite.

Lili Mae spots the blackbird and its mate. I feel a surge of joy.

Down by the twin oak I announce my presence by pressing on the bark. I sit on the bench. I feel no energy coming from the tree, but the profound silence engulfs me. Here, we are closer to the road. A motorbike rips through the velvet stillness.

Then distant, excited voices. The air is suddenly alive with it. Things are loosening up. We are allowed out.

I get up, close and lock the gate.

Dry

Lee and I have plans to cross the river and inspect the groves of trees we planted there thirty years ago. Sheep graze the forty acres not occupied by trees. We built a sword bridge, so-called because it is so narrow that one swordsman could defend it against an army.

Finally, we decide to make an initial tour by car. We have had little rain and the earth is hard and dry, so we unlock the gate in the little side road that leads to Castlekevin where our retired, much-missed Daniel Day-Lewis lives.

Sean Nolan grazes his sheep here but they are elsewhere at present as he hopes to make a little hay before he brings them back.

I bought this piece of land from Rosie Rochford after her father, the farmer, died, and immediately set out to plant it with trees. We planted twenty-one borders and groves with several thousand trees.

As an aside, there are several Rochfords living in Annamoe, French Protestants who fled to Ireland to escape the Inquisition. They are now, and have been for many generations, devout Catholics. Just as the Palestinians were probably the Jews who stayed, later forcibly converted to Islam. So it goes.

Lee and I toured the tree plantations, and I was relieved that most were in vigorous good health. I had neglected them since my feet gave up on me, but Lee shares my love of trees and he will take over their custody. We decided to return tomorrow (Sunday) to investigate more thoroughly.

A developer friend of mine said, before the crash of 2008, 'I go to bed rich and I wake up richer.'

I said, 'My trees don't grow during the night, but they sometimes put on 5 mm during the day.'

Heavily overcast this morning,
but the sun making a contest of it

We cross the river again, this time by the sword bridge. The river is sluggish, so little rain.

Yesterday we inspected the trees planted all around the periphery to give our borders a rich deep curtain. Today we start by investigating the one exception to the general good health, an oak grove where the leaves are burnt and shrivelled. Is it a virus? Is it possible that it could infect all our other oaks? Distressingly, it keeps reminding Lee and me of this other virus. After taking some advice we find it is not too serious. A good fall of rain will wash out the mildew and the trees will make another crop of leaves.

We planted a series of groves on both sides of the grass walkway leading down to the humpback bridge from the house. The bridge crosses the little Moneystown river that empties into our Avonmore river. We built a pagoda where the two rivers meet, but it got swept away by a flood. The confluence is thought to be magical, but we have found it violent and wishing to be left alone.

One of the most awesome sights that the planet has to offer is in Manaus, Brazil, where the Rio Negro violently collides with the Amazon as the two rivers vie for supremacy, the black and green waters churning together. I once swam in that turbulent confluence, the now broken old man who nervously dips into the swimming hole.

Overcast, but mild this morning

Happily, rain is expected at last. It is Monday and Lee is back at work online. The walk across the river is daunting and will have to wait till next weekend when he is free. I will resume my wander down the drive and visit my friends. Many of them were planted by Dr Sam Synge, brother of the poet J.M. Synge. Dr Sam was the rector here in the 1920s, just a hundred years ago. The exotica, like the monkey puzzle and the redwoods, appear to be a hundred years old, as do the fifteen limes. They would suggest that he kept bees for lime-blossom honey, which is exquisite, clear and fragrant.

When I arrived here half a century ago I got to know Dr Sam Synge's son, John, then in his seventies. He was born in this house. He told me that his father had been a medical missionary in China and had studied Chinese medicine. He was famous for his sermons, which never exceeded five minutes. It sounded as though he got more from the Chinese than they got from him. I am so indebted to him for all the trees he planted and to the subsequent incumbents for not cutting them down. I feel a strong connection to Dr Sam.

I take my walk. The air is moist, but no rain yet. The elders are coated in flowers. I always have the intention of making elderflower cordial, but never quite get round to it.

As a servant to the trees I have become woefully inadequate. Trees cast a spell on us. They make us love them and serve them. I felt guilty about not thinning the trees in the groves, but I discovered they thin themselves quite successfully. The weaker trees cannot reach the canopy and so perish. I walk on.

Even the thorns are sporting a few straggly blossoms. The gunnera's big flat leaves squat on the ground and rot away all winter. Any day now they will start resurrecting. Flowers are popping up all over.

Overcast this morning, mild, no wind

On the right-hand side of the drive, opposite the Great Oak, are two aspens; their 'quaking' leaves flutter in the slightest breeze and in a high wind they become hysterical. When people believed the wind was the Holy Ghost they must have watched the quaking aspen with apprehension. Aspens leaf late so I was not alarmed when no buds appeared, but I was when white stripe fungus appeared on the lower trunk of one of them. We have a fallen tree covered with white stripe fungus. I call it the Undertaker. As soon as I saw those stripes I knew it was dead. I watched the other aspen anxiously and was relieved when it started budding. I fear they have been starved of sunlight. I must do a little trimming of the trees behind them.

I went out late. The morning clouds have gone, a warm breeze from the south east, blossom everywhere. A lovely summer's day. My daughter Daisy tells me that London is hot and humid and oppressive.

Heavy cloud cover this morning

What a contrast. Feels like night. Still no rain. Those clouds are constipated.

I lay awake last night. The room was hot and sleep would not come. I started fretting over the GREAT MYSTERY. How does all that water get up to the top of the tree? We know that the taproot can reach down to the water table for water. It must have some kind of suction device to get the water up and pump it upwards. Then the revelation came. What if all those theories are right? Capillary action, H_3O^+, vacuum of the leaves. What if they all play a part? Yes, it is a team effort. The great mystery is solved! With that thought, I was able to fall asleep at last.

No cloud cover this morning

The sun shot an early salvo through my east-facing bedroom window. I wasn't so sure about having solved the great mystery in the glare of the morning sun.

I took my electric Zimmer to look at the four ash trees Lee transplanted. Two are sturdy and doing well. The others died. I wanted to examine their bark, which had been eaten by deer. A tree can live if some portion of the bark survives.

Between the trunk and the bark is the cambium layer. This is where all the action is, both up and down. Water and sap go up and carbon molecules go down. The leaves make the carbon, pass it on to a twig; a twig to a branch, branch to trunk and the clever cambium passes the carbon on to the tree for growth. How the carbon molecules get into the trunk we don't know, but the trunk would be porous enough to grant them entry. Imagine the volume of carbon being produced by a hundred thousand leaves, and how tiny these fragments are. Is the subconscious the controlling force of salvation for them here too? A tree can survive with 10 per cent of its cambium intact. The bark of the two ash trees was stripped all the way round. There was no hope of salvation for them.

The brisk S E wind is appearing to be blowing the sluggish river backwards. Wispy clouds are gathering. I take a walk. All looks well.

Wind

Rained in the night, heavily and happily. And wind. The eight-stemmed sycamore fills my south-facing bedroom window. It was shaking and blowing and rustling all night. Wind shaking leaves stimulates growth, though no growth happens at night. The sun's energy is required.

Charles Darwin delayed publishing his magnum opus for many years because of the effect it would have on his devout wife. Their conversation might have gone something like this:

> 'Darling, I have some bad news. God didn't create the world. It came about through natural selection.'
> 'Don't be silly, Charles, I'm off to take Communion.'
> 'Do you really believe that wafer is actually the flesh of Christ?'
> 'Of course I do. Why are you crying, Charles?'

We count the rings on a felled tree to tell its age, the assumption being that the tree goes on growing, although oaks don't appear to grow after a hundred years or so; yet they sport leaves, so photosynthesis goes on, separating the carbon from carbon dioxide, and the carbon fragments continue to rain down to the cambium layer. What does it do with them? Does it coax the tree, *Come on, take your carbon*, or let it drain away?

Although I have studied trees all my life, I gather knowledge from observation rather than science. I am a curious amateur.

Just as a baby swallow knows how to fly alone to Africa, a tree knows what to do at any stage of its life cycle. This supports my belief that a force like our subconscious is running things; human, animal and plant. Christians would say that is God. Scientists would call it natural selection.

I take a walk. From here, high by the house, I can see the astonishing curve of the Great Oak's dense and luxuriant fan of leaves.

I walk down the hill and examine my humble thorn bushes. Perhaps encouraged by all my attention, they have thrown out new branches – well, twigs really – with unbecoming exuberance, some intruding on the driveway. Judicious pruning is called for.

*Very windy. Prevailing SW wind
bringing much-needed rain*

Last weekend Lee and I explored the trees we planted around the periphery of the land across the river. They were mostly healthy. I am hoping that the welcome rain that has fallen over the last two days has washed the mildew off the 'burned' oak leaves.

Our focus this weekend is on the groves on either side of the walkway leading to the humpback bridge on the main road. We had to cross the sword bridge first. Lee wheeled me down to the river. I leaned on Lili while Lee carried the wheelchair over the bridge. He came back and carried me up the steps and I walked across the bridge, clutching the handrail. Lee helped me down the step on the other side.

The plan was to examine the groves on the right-hand side of the walkway, and on the left-hand side on the way back. Many of these groves are enormous and thousands of trees were involved. Lee pushed me for three and a half hours over rough ground, and as we got closer to the humpback bridge the ground became swampier and the going got even harder for Lee, my unbeaten cage-fighter, lawyer son. I will sort out my notes and report on each grove tomorrow.

The sun is shining and the wild SW wind has dropped

The grove numbers below correspond to a map that hangs in the house.

16: A small beech wood, strong and healthy. All the groves were fenced against the sheep, but the deer could have jumped the sheep fence, although there is no evidence of their depredations in any of the groves. About 300 trees.

15: Sessile oak, white willow, holly. No sign of the holly, which is usually tenacious. We have a few ancient holly trees. It is interesting that above grazing height there are no prickles on the leaves. The willows are doing well, which is pleasing since they don't much like our acid soil. The oaks are dominant. About 400 trees.

12: Common alder, golden willow, coral bark willow. I have neglected thinning, but the trees have taken care of that themselves. The weaker trees can't reach the light, so their whitened bodies scatter the floor of the groves. One desperate alder shot a horizontal branch 15 ft out of the grove; it saw light, tipped upward and leafed. About 600 trees.

11: Beech, birch, alder. A long grove and dense. The canopy is filled. It is dark and mysterious. About 500 trees.

10: Pedunculated oak, silvery birch, downy birch, aspen, weeping willow. A huge grove. No sign of weeping willow. It was a Chinese import in the eighteenth century. It does not thrive in this soil. I am delighted the aspens are doing so well. They leaf late and I was afraid all the airspace would have been

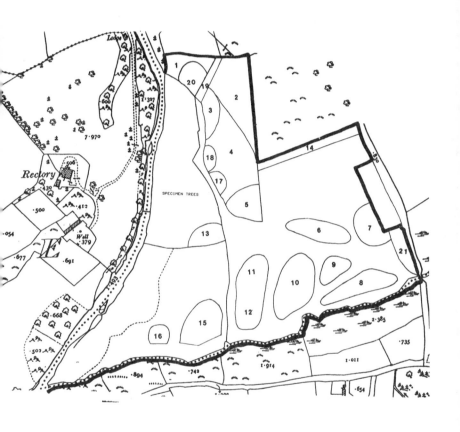

John Boorman's Native Broadleaved Woodlands, Annamoe, Co. Wicklow.

taken, but they are up there holding their own. Their leaves are quaking frantically in this high wind.

9: Aspen. A whole grove to itself. Only the outer trees are quaking. Trees baffle the wind. When you walk in a wood you are gifted calm. A cure for anxiety. I have always been intrigued by the aspen. At the time, I insisted they had a grove to themselves. I didn't think they could compete. About 500 trees.

8: Beech, white willow, golden willow. A small grove to bring us to the humpback bridge. Now we go back the other way. About 400 trees.

7: A few firs and lots of oaks: Douglas firs, pedunculated oak. About 200 trees.

6: Beech. Such a beautiful tree, not indigenous but a welcome immigrant. There is a mature beech wood that climbs a hill just across from the swimming hole. About 400 trees.

5: Sessile oak, common ash. The lovely ash is not so common. It is hunted down by a deadly virus, as are we. The ash and I will hide out here together, hidden by the oaks. About 500 trees.

17: Hornbeam. I love it. Also known as ironwood. The hardest of all woods and it has a grove all to itself. About 250 trees.

18: Downey birch and golden birch. This brings us back to the house and completes the overhung walkway. About 600 trees.

We then went to examine the grove of oaks with the 'burned' leaves. The heavy rain had washed away the mildew, but it still looked sad.

There are still groves we have not looked at. I will come back to them another time.

Of the forty acres, about half are now woodlands.

The sun beats down out of a white-hot sky

Lee returned from his early-morning walk with his dog, bearing the news that we have lost an oak. I went down right away. Thankfully it was not one of the ancient chorus of hundred-year-old ones that are rooted along the top of the slope. It was planted halfway down. Its leaves were healthy and moist, but its broken trunk was wet and mushy. The wood crumbled in your hands. It looked like the work of a malicious fungus. We set about burning it in case it spreads.

It later clouded over.

A warm, sunny day

Lee cut the nail on my typing finger this morning. When the finger pressed a key, the nail hit the one above the finger. He has promised to cut the other nails when he has more time. One more thing I can no longer do for myself.

The news is all about Dominic Cummings breaking the lockdown rule. Boris's support, as ever, is about himself. If he lost Cummings he would have to do all the things prime ministers do. Corbyn rightly called him a part-time prime minister. Boris has declared that he intends to take paternity leave soon. Leave it all to Dominic. The Conservatives have spent ten years cutting money from the NHS, but take no blame for its impoverishment.

> For years right-wing Tory toffs,
> Squeezed life out of the NHS,
> For they had private medicine,
> Just as their private schools,
> Sucked life from state ones.
> When the nation clapped the NHS,
> The noise was so profound,
> It may bring Eton crashing down.

Here in Ireland the politicians are being clearer and safer. In the UK the class system always simmers just below the surface. Please forgive my rant: I feel closer to Ireland and to my Irish children and to Europe and further away from England.

I went down and looked at the fallen oak, its leaves wilted and dying. Sad sight in the midst of such rejoicing life, its broken trunk smouldering.

I visited the twin oak and stroked its bark to announce my arrival. The signals coming from the tree were strong and consoling. My anger and sorrow melted away. Those are not emotions for an old man approaching the end of his life.

Warm, sunny day

I have asked Lili Mae to take some photos as prompts for Sue Morley's illustrations of this account, including the stone with its Celtic spirals.

Brother Anthony, a monk from Glenstal Abbey, spent many weeks carving it, and just as a Renaissance artist would say *Pope Pious the Whatsit caused this to be made*, so Brother Anthony carved into the stone, *John Boorman caused this to be made*. He carved it in Ogham, so few people will be able to read his modest inscription. I would like to affirm that it is all his own laborious work. The Celtic spirals are particularly difficult to carve since they are continuous curves. If he had sinned, this was a perfect penance. My only contribution was to feed him while he carved.

I affirm the stone is his. If, one day, he turns up with a large lorry he is free to take it away. Brother Anthony is also a knowledgeable forester who advised me on my tree-planting.

28 MAY

Yet another warm, sunny day

During April I was alarmed that although buttercups were showing, there were no daisies. With all these viruses about, imagine a world without daisies. I have a daughter, Daisy. I want to reassure the reader that daisies have now appeared in huge numbers as never before, as though they heard about me doubting them. If the daisy were rare, it would be prized, but since it overpopulates, it is undervalued.

We have always had a few dragonflies at the swimming hole, but now, Lee tells me, we have a squadron of them flitting among the yellow irises. No flies or nits or midges yet, they come in August, but Lili Mae found a ladybird.

As I walk down I notice that a bird is singing in both thorn bushes. The second bush has a crown of blossom, the first bush has not.

What astonishes and humbles me is the profusion and complexity of nature. We cannot know it, only bend a knee before it. A hospital will have sixty specialists, each confining themselves to one aspect of the human body. The human physiognomy is a tiny fragment of the whole of nature.

My friend Clodagh, who runs the shop in Laragh, the next village along, says that the blackbird pecking at my window was pecking at his own reflection, which he takes to be a rival bird. When I see an old man peering at me from the mirror I am shocked, for inside I am still a shiny young film director.

An old man slumps down on the bench by the twin oak. I am at the outer limit of my world. Last weekend's excursion into the groves across the river feels like a visit to another galaxy.

It was hot out there. I was dehydrated, and overheated. It took me a while to plod back.

Another hot day, but a cooling breeze

The blowsy, eight-stemmed sycamore continues its assault on the implacable redwoods. I learn that the redwood's abrasive needles are not only fireproof but also function as lightning conductors. The redwoods are in a class of their own. The giant redwoods in northern California are a sight to behold. As we stare up at them in wonderment, we ask again: how do they get water hundreds of feet up to the top of those monsters? My tentative suggestion that it might be a team effort sounds paltry when confronted by those giants.

I stop at the first thorn bush, perfectly lined up with the groves leading to the humpback bridge. It is pleasing to the eye. The trees overhang the walkway in perfect symmetry. Thank you, Jeremy Williams, the landscape architect who laid out the plan, and thank you, Brother Anthony.

Further down I was glad to see the aspen quaking away in this wind.

I pass the fallen oak, its broken trunk still smouldering. Before a tree drops its leaves in the autumn, it withdraws all the valuable nitrogen. In this case the leaves have died with the nitrogen intact so they become a valuable gift to lay at the feet of an oak.

I reach the twin oak, my destination. Beyond it is the gate to the outer world. I touch the bark to announce my presence. I sit on the bench and watch the river. The low branches touch the water.

Once again I am dissolving into everything around me.

I am of no consequence.

A warm, sunny day with an easterly breeze to cool us off

This continuous warm, sunny weather is forcing the summer upon us before we are quite ready for it. When I was making *Deliverance*, we started up in the hills in Clayton, Georgia ('Where spring spends the summer'). We could put that sign up in Annamoe, but not this year.

As I step out of the conservatory door, I sense that the beginning of a dark green heaviness is upon us. The chestnut's blossoms have gone and its candles are drooping. The dying sycamore continues its shameless cycle of dying and resurrection.

The last few days of riotous blossom and luminous green leaves are gone. Even the gorse on the hill is not as chrome yellow as it was. However, the elder is hanging in there. There is so much blossom the tree is obliterated. Still up by the house, the Great Oak's lofty fan of rich darkening leaves crowns it all. I walk on down, and I must admit, it is good to feel the sun on my back.

31 MAY

Warm and sunny

On this, the last day of this beautiful month of May, I want to salute the trees that have been my constant companions throughout these two months.

With Lee's heroic help I was at last able to put my arms around the huge girth of the Great Oak.

My two prickly thorn bushes that I tease, and they maliciously tease me.

I salute the huge ambition of the brash, eight-stemmed sycamore wanting to be the biggest tree of all.

The silent, soaring redwoods, wearing their needles like chain mail.

The cluster of four limes. When I stand enfolded in their leafy midst, it is like being embraced by nature herself.

The monstrous, overgrown larch, its branches wandering at will, is now given some semblance of shape by being clothed in a cloak of green needles.

Finally, the noble twin oak, who probably knows everything: if only she would speak, or teach me her language. I keep hoping, and sometimes knowing.

Yet another warm, sunny day as the lockdown eases

Stepping out this morning I am reminded of the small, rich world I inhabit. I notice the dying sycamore, whose healthy crop of leaves shows it has pulled its death-defying trick yet again. The oak I planted by the carved boulder is flourishing. To the right of the steep hill that announces Annamoe, the upper branches of my majestic Great Oak display a rich arch of dense leaves.

The four limes across the driveway are leafed from trunk to lofty height with vibrant leaves that threaten to overdose me on oxygen. Then a great curve of the river opens up. On the other side of the river are the many groves of trees Lee and I recently explored that take the eye to a humpback bridge that marks our boundary. The driveway then passes under the birch arch.

The Great Oak is 70 yards away and I have long regretted that I could not cross that rough ground on my pusher but Lee heroically carried me across and up the slope so that I could finally put my arms across the tree's great girth.

It is very warm. Lee proposes to take me down to the swimming hole. I climb on his back and he carries me into deeper water and I slide into my beloved river. We swim across to the Rock of Truth. The water is warm, as it seldom is. It is magic. We swim into all its crooks and corners. We wallow in it.

We dry off in the sun. We name the wild native trees on the riverbank – ash, birch, alder and rowan.

2 JUNE

Yet another sun-drenched day, but rain promised later

We hear the distant, plaintive call of the cuckoo, the harbinger of summer. It reassures us that summer may be some way off, but it is coming.

Two years ago a cuckoo perched in a tree just outside my kitchen door. Its cry at close quarters is harsh and ear-splitting. It revealed the cuckoo for what it really is, a lazy thief. A natural-history cameraman friend of mine nursed the ambition to actually photograph a cuckoo laying its egg. He tried for several years, but always just missed it. What he did capture was the cuckoo watching the little birds building their nest; she watched them attentively as they laid their eggs, but it was in the fifth year of my friend's attempts that he finally photographed the cuckoo laying her egg in the nest.

The cuckoo waited until both birds left the nest. I saw the final result. She dived in, laid her egg and left. I held the 35mm film in my hands. It was over in thirteen frames of film. There are twenty-five frames per second, so it took just over half a second. In due course the eggs hatched and the young cuckoo pushed the other chicks out of the nest, and the two tiny birds kept bringing the cuckoo chick lots to eat.

The moral being that intelligence and cunning beat hard work and ignorance any day. It is hard to fathom how natural selection came up with this one.

Cold and windy. Rain

At last rain is falling onto parched earth. We had almost no rain in April and May.

This planet should be called Water, not Earth. There is much more water than earth. Like most other animals we are made mostly of water. We need a constant supply of it to keep us alive. We were creatures of the sea who crept onto the earth and have never quite evolved. We need water. We are always gasping for it. When an Irishman goes down to the pub every night for a pint, he is just topping up. What keeps this precarious system going is that water cheats. It does not obey the laws of physics that apply to everything else, like it expands when it gets colder instead of the other way round.

Whether it was God or evolution working this thing out, it was necessary to break the rules in order to make it all work. For instance, why is water vapour lighter than air, and why does it remain as vapour when it gets higher and colder? Don't ask, it is too embarrassing. It stays up there in the cold air as vapour, as cloud.

Thankfully the rules are broken for our benefit. I suspect not too much rain has fallen yet. The earth is still parched.

4 JUNE

Heavy cloud cover and only light rain

I venture out. The air is moist and still. The lightest of rain caresses the face.

I walk down the driveway and see that the spindly fern stalks have shot up overnight. They will soon reach 6 ft in height and put out those beautiful, fan-like palm leaves. They don't procreate like other plants. They come from an earlier stage of evolution, before sex was invented. They grow from spores, not seeds.

When I first came to Ireland I asked what people used to fertilize their potatoes before artificial fertilizers, and nobody could tell me. Finally, I came across an old man who told me that they used ferns, which are rich in potassium and grow in profusion on the hills.

Lee tells me that a good crop of little apples is forming in the walled garden. We planted a new orchard of apples three years ago and it is now bearing fruit. We have always had a crab-apple tree, which blossoms effusively. Its apples are small and bitter. It is the only indigenous apple. All the species we enjoy have been grafted on to the bitter crab apple. It demonstrates that immigrants can be nicer than natives.

The last shot of *Excalibur* is of Arthur's body being taken by boat to Avalon, the land of the apple. The legend has it that he will return in the hour of England's greatest need. That must be about now. Perhaps he will appear as an Apple Inc. device that brings peace and harmony.

Wilding is a kind of democracy of the earth.
Let everything grow, wild flowers and weeds alike.
I have embraced it before it had a name, out of idleness.

WEEDS

We have cut you and mowed you,
Uprooted and sprayed you,
Tried to eliminate you,
Ethnically cleansed you,
Kept our lawns free of you,
But our crimes have been listed,
Underground warfare persisted,
Wilding has made us admit our mistakes,
We regret our cruelty and hate,
Wilding has taught us to love.
Welcome back dear dandelion.
Come home purple thistle.
Feel safe yellow ragwort.
Rejoice golden gorse.
Whatever your colour or race,
You can now safely show your face.

The sun is shining this morning.
It rained in the night, but not enough

Lili Mae walked with me this morning. She brought along her book in case it got boring. With her sharper eye she spotted two rabbits and a wild flower I didn't recognize. There is cloud about but it is fluffy, white cumulus, not dark and rain-bearing.

I have written before of how my beloved twin oak hangs precariously over the river as she seeks morning light, for the line of oaks above her takes all the afternoon light. She has developed stratagems to deal with this. She allows the low branches on the riverside to flourish, since they don't pull as the higher ones do. This is why it is so crowded low down and why so many branches dangle in the river. The leaves need a constant supply of water and are consequently heavy. I have presented the various theories, but no one knows how our Great Oak gets 150 gallons of water up to its leaves every day.

Now the twin oak has come up with a new trick. She has sent out a substantial branch low down along the river bank. Once it clears all the other low branches it does a 90-degree turn and heads for the river and its light. It is now spurting out leaves into empty air.

Which part of the tree makes these decisions? Is it the straining roots? Or the leaves? Yes, the leaves. Every leaf is conducting a photosynthesis dance with the sun. It is sensitive to light and time. While it is still a bud, it is probably deciding when to leaf. It may be calculating the weight of the riverside of the tree.

Lee is summoned to work in his office in Dublin next week. He will have to put on his suit and tie. Our sun-drenched idyll is over and storm clouds are coming. I shall have to go back to my carers with the attendant risk of infection, even though the infection level in Ireland is low. My precious Lili Mae will stay as long as lockdown is enforced.

It is five years ago today that my friend and neighbour, Paolo Tullio, died. He knew everything. I miss him still.

Rain overnight and raining this morning

Wind from the prevailing SW. I will wait for the rain to ease before I set out.

The sun is making a late, watery appearance. I walk down to the twin oak. As always, I stroke the bark to announce my arrival.

I sit on the bench and watch the slow-moving river. The sun dapples the light on the fluttering oak leaves. My mind slowly empties of thought. I feel a sense of peace.

Gradually, something coming from the tree fills my emptiness. It is changing me. I am becoming liquid. I drain into the soil under the bench. I am sucked into the tree.

A fat raindrop falls on my face and wakes me up.

7 JUNE

Overcast

I have been waiting for the promised sun, but I go out without it.

The eight-stemmed sycamore continues to burgeon. It is vast and unapologetic. It leans on the redwoods, making vulgar fun of their aloofness. About thirty years ago, I planted another redwood. It climbed more than 40 ft before putting out a leaf, and now finally it has found some airspace and it is growing leaves for the first time.

I walk down through the four lime trees to the thorn bushes. I remember as a child, during the Second World War, eating their leaves. We used to call it the cheese tree because its leaves tasted vaguely of cheese. Cheese was rationed so we felt we were winning by eating the cheese leaves.

Will the post-virus world be more modest? Will we look back on the supermarket as the high point of the previous era? Will Lee and Lili tell their children how the supermarket contained thousands of foods coming from all parts of the world, and that you could go into the supermarket from week to week, confident that the items you require will be on the same shelves? It was a miracle of technology, organization, packaging and shipping. Container ships and planes, fleets of trucks and huge amounts of fossil fuels were all involved in providing these items. We were known as 'consumers'. Will the next generation be modest? Will they grow their own food as they struggle to pay back those huge debts?

8 JUNE

Bright, sunny morning

One day soon, the lime trees will blossom. We have fifteen of these beautiful trees that leaf their trunks as well as their branches. Every day I pause under the cluster of four limes on our driveway and listen for the roaring of the bees. Not yet, but soon. According to John Synge, his father, Dr Sam Synge, was a beekeeper and interested in the curative qualities of lime-blossom honey.

I walk out into a landscape that has changed. The blossom has all disappeared. The birdsong has largely disappeared too, except for the mournful wood pigeon. The other birds have successfully found their mates and are busy building nests. The leaves have lost their bright freshness.

Summer is here.

9 JUNE

Heavy cloud cover

This morning as I walked out, looking at my trees that I keep like pets, I was reminded of the six months I spent in the Amazon, the greatest forest in the world, preparing and making *The Emerald Forest*. It was an experience that profoundly changed me. I came to understand that this is a tree planet, and we cannot survive without them.

I spent some time living with a tribe in the Xingu, a vast area unknown to the outside world until 1947. The relationship of the indigenous people with nature was so seamlessly integrated that it made me realize just how far away we have strayed. The brutal devastation of clear-felling, contrasted with men praying to a tree they were about to cut down. The problem is that there are too many of us. When there are more people than trees in the world, we are in trouble.

We read reports of the Amazon rainforest being clear-felled, and the impression given is that the rainforest is disappearing. In fact it is such a vast area, like the Pacific Ocean, that huge amounts of it remain, as the following story will show.

I was looking for locations for *The Emerald Forest*, flying in a light aircraft. We encountered an electrical storm that the plane was ill-equipped to pass through, so we had to fly around it. We were pushed further and further away from our destination. We were running short of fuel. I was sitting next to the pilot, searching the forest for some clearing or town, but we flew for two hours over endless forest without discovering a clearing. I said to the pilot, 'Could we land on the canopy, the dense forest surface?' He replied that we certainly could land on the canopy, but we would be stuck up there, since we would be 50 or 60 ft above the ground. We had no idea where we were so it was hopeless to radio for help. The fuel gauge was showing empty. At long last we saw a clearing. It was a football pitch. We landed. I had finally located where 'the middle of nowhere' was.

Another dull start. Rain expected

I walk down, checking on the trees. No sign of bees in the limes; the Great Oak's immensity stunning as ever, planted 30 ft below the other mature oaks, but towering above them.

I take a look at the fallen oak. The white stripes of fungi are all over it. Where do they come from? How do they identify a dead tree from a living one? We know that just as we have enzymes in our mouths and stomachs to break down foods, so the fungi have tough enzymes that break down wood into food they can eat. How do they identify dead wood from live wood? I suspect they do have a go at the living, but the tree exudes something nasty to discourage them.

Here we see Darwin's theory at work. Everything is trying to kill everything else, or eat everything else, and only the strongest survive.

> Mrs Darwin: 'What an ugly way of looking at things. Nature is beautiful, Charles.'

One could take a more benign view of the fungi chomping away at the dead tree, and say this is nature cleaning up after herself. Darwin would consider that to be anthropomorphic nonsense.

> Mrs Darwin: 'Oh, do look on the bright side for once, Charles.'

It has started to rain. I should hurry home, except of course, I cannot hurry. I stop trying and just get gloriously wet.

11 JUNE

Wind and rain this morning

The eight-stemmed sycamore fills my south-facing bedroom window, and this morning it was being shaken alarmingly by a bullying wind. It squeaked and groaned and cried out. These multiple stems are spindly compared to, say, the stolid oak. One large bunch of leaves was being flung against another. One felt it was being chastised for overambition.

There is a wonderful public walk from Luggala to Loch Dan and when you reach your destination you may rest under the shade of a huge sycamore. The last time I was there, before my legs left me, it had fallen, apparently no longer able to support its own enormous weight.

12 JUNE

Broken clouds and wind

One of the greatest pleasures nature has to offer is the sight of swallows wheeling and dancing in the wind, high up in the heavens, as they were performing this afternoon.

Mrs Darwin would clap her hands in delight while Charles would point out:

> 'They have evolved into insect-hunters. They are acting out of hunger, not pleasure.'
> 'Oh Charles, you're such a spoilsport.'

It reminded me of a day during the Battle of Britain, when high up in a clear blue sky we watched a dogfight between a Spitfire and a Messerschmitt. They wheeled and twisted, but there was no sound. They were too high up. Finally, the German plane fell in smoke and flames. We clapped and cheered. The Spitfire dipped and did a victory roll.

'Wasn't it wonderful,' said my mother, 'they were like a pair of swallows.'

Wet and windy. Sun later

Many, perhaps all of our decisions are made by our subconscious. We observe the effects of imprinted behaviour in animals, such as migration, or a bird knowing which berries are poisonous.

> 'How do you explain that one, Charles?'
> 'Thousands of birds died eating that berry. The birds that survived were the ones that did not eat the berry. Eventually it became imprinted.'
> 'Who did the imprinting, Charles?'
> 'Time, darling. Trial and error over thousands of years.'
> 'Wrong, Charles, it was God.'

Is it possible that our subconscious is part of a web of forces influencing the behaviour of all plants and animals?

Take the human animal. It has consciousness, which tells it to nourish this complex body we live in but do not understand. It obliges us to spend a third of our lives unconscious. We don't know why. This body we inhabit will wear out and die. We cannot grasp the concept of extinction, nor of eternity. We can enjoy a sense of peaceful well-being while racing around the sun at 30 km per second. We are gifted illusionists.

The beauty and mystery of nature consoles us, but only laughter and a sense of the absurd can sustain us.

Sun this morning and fresh smell to the air after the storm

We had a storm last night, thunder and lightning. I described earlier encountering one in the Amazon, where they are frequent and violent. The weather pattern in the rainforest is that each day you get a thunderstorm followed by torrential rain. This rain is so intense that it is impossible to go out in it. It is like standing under a waterfall. You make an appointment by saying, 'I will meet you after the rain.' It will go on for an hour and then the rest of the day is powerful sunshine.

A rain cloud gets charged up with electricity, positive on top of the cloud and negative at the bottom. No one seems to know how electricity gets up there, unless I am missing something. When top and bottom collide we get a huge charge of lightning, which has to find somewhere to discharge. A 300-year-old oak would have a good chance of being hit through its sheer longevity.

The leaves of the redwoods, besides being fireproof, are also conductors that can deflect lightning to earth. The redwoods are set for the duration. Only a man with a chainsaw can truncate this journey from a thousand years ago.

Bright sun woke me at six this morning

On this warm and sunny day, exactly halfway through the month, I decided to make an inventory of the trees and plants in my care.

The chestnut is producing a crop of conkers. Some little ones have dropped from the tree. Its branches are beginning to be weighed down by its fruit. The beech that stands next to it has put on some weight already and is very large indeed, and loaded with beechnuts.

The dying sycamore has pulled its old trick and produced a massive roof of dazzling leaves. He shall be spared for another year.

The rock with Celtic spirals looks rather diminished by the oak I planted next to it, but the whitebeam on its other side is a magical companion and reminds us of all our ancestors.

The big tall Scots pine is looking well and its high swing most inviting. Next to it is the great fan of leaves, the crown of the Great Oak. Its majesty rules the world.

I work my way down the hill. The ambitious eight-stemmed sycamore is reaching up, trying to obliterate the redwoods. They, however quietly reach for the heavens. Then we come to the lime trees. We're still awaiting the bees that will follow the blossom.

The arc of the river comes into view. It is running higher from all the rain. My first thorn bush is showing three pathetic blossoms, rather late in the day. I pause there because it offers a splendid view of the groves across the river. Lee went over there at the weekend and I was delighted to learn that the cluster of infected oaks have recovered and are showing new leaves.

The groves are beginning to mark the passage to the humpback bridge, which seems a humble destination for this noble avenue.

The humpback bridge looks a little embarrassed at not being the Arc de Triomphe. Lee gave me a piggyback to the Great Oak yesterday and I marvelled at it once again. It is bigger and healthier than any old oak I have ever seen anywhere.

The Great Oak, and the line of oaks on the slope, are invaded by hazel bushes that climb to the tops of the trees, obscuring them. The hazels are wispy and vague, they lack structure and depend on the oaks for support. Are they choking their hosts? Should I cut them back?

On the right of the driveway, the aspens have their leaves fluttering in the slightest breeze, and the overgrown larch continues to sprawl in all directions.

I see the fungi are busily eating the fallen oak. They must have the toughest enzymes. I wonder if they suffer from indigestion.

We come to the twin oak that leans precariously over the river. I sit on the bench and think about my relationship with these trees. I look after them and they, in turn, take care of me.

Cloudy start, but the sun breaks through

Collecting ferns was fashionable in Victorian times; people even had ferneries in which to display them. I owe another debt to my predecessors, for the many ferns that I keep discovering over the years.

The tall, spindly ones near the twin oak have now climbed up to 6 or 7 ft and have a new roof of beautiful leaves. By contrast, I have also found ferns that cling to the earth and then spread out to a floor of complex patterns.

They are a memory of how the world looked when it was unobserved.

'Full many a flower is born to blush unseen'
–Thomas Gray

Ferns grow from spores, not seeds, from a time before sex was invented, but now I learn that even then there was some male–female thing involved.

There are so many tall ferns at the swimming hole that you almost need a compass to find your way in. In August, flies as dense as locusts invade. If you put a sprig of fern in each ear it keeps the flies away, or at least at bay. They swarm close to the surface of the river and fish jump to catch them; in the evening the bats swoop down to blindly gobble them up, and still the flies keep coming. They want your earwax and the salty moisture in the corner of your eyes. They seem mad from hunger and yet so adroit at escaping death by swatting.

How often I have aimed at them but slapped myself.

Cloud and sun taking turns

Another angry thunderstorm last night. The rain was so intense it stopped the traffic. Drivers could not see. It reminded me of the Amazon, 'I will meet you after the rain.' Storm rules: keep your head down till it's over. Stay in the air-raid shelter till the siren sounds the all-clear.

The air is crisp and clean this morning. A few heavy drops of rain fall on my head, highly-charged leftovers from the storm. The swollen river is running the rain away.

I am sure the twin oak is the dryad, the mistress of the oaks, but she is shaken by the storm. Do trees have a fear of lightning – the one thing, together with the chain saw, that can end their lives? All the trees look limp and crestfallen this morning. Me too.

> Trees are,
> I am not,
> They speak,
> I cannot hear.
> They live on,
> I will die.

Cloud persists, but the sun is having none of it

It comes bustling out with all the confidence of the solstice only a few days away.

The trees are lush with leaves. They have lost that first bright rapture and have darkened as they get down to work.

Leaves make sucrose in summer, which the tree stores during winter. Sucrose mixes with water, which is then pumped up from the roots and sent up to the buds, encouraging them to become leaves.

Every leaf then becomes a chemical factory through photosynthesis, separating carbon dioxide into oxygen, which it expels back into the air, and carbon, which it sends down to the tree. It also produces carbohydrates, which the tree stores as sugar, and the whole cycle begins again.

Yet nothing explains why and how water rises so vigorously from the roots before the buds have become leaves. Is it another case of water not obeying maths. Mathematics was discovered, not invented, so someone, up there or back then, let water off the hook.

The month continues to send down much-needed rain

Some kind of energy field around the twin oak draws creatures to it. Lately, I have seen three rabbits convening a meeting by the tree. I hope they are the same three rabbits every day. For every rabbit you see, there are ten that you don't.

I noted last month that the birdsong by the twin oak was deeper, suggesting bigger birds. Perhaps all these creatures, like me, are drawn to a soothing and healing energy field.

Sun probing me out of bed very early

Almost solstice. There is light at 4 am. And still at 10 pm.

Some years ago I took Lee to the Midnight Sun Film Festival in Finland where we had that disconcerting experience of the missing night. The sun appears to be setting, but it skims along the horizon, then starts rising again. We miss the mystery of darkness, of dreams, of renewal, of the possibility of starting afresh. I recall those all-night parties of my youth, of wandering into the new day like a stranger. Our grip on this planet is slender enough without foregoing our footholds.

Meanwhile, the redwood leaves don't fall, fulfilling all the functions of a leaf as well as protecting the tree from fire and lightning.

> 'Charles, you clever Dick, what does your theory say about that poor larch in the garden?'
> 'What is troubling you, Mrs Darwin?'
> 'Well, it is a pine that sheds its needles in September. So is it a pine trying to be a leafy tree, or is it a leafy tree trying to be a pine?'
> 'We shall see, Mrs Darwin.'
> 'When?'

The solstice

The sun will be directly overhead at noon, but we may not see it. There is heavy cloud cover.

Lee was back from his office for the weekend and pushed me in the wheelchair across the bridge to inspect the groves. We went from one to another, in each case deeply affected by the atmosphere in each wood. It was calming and peaceful. These forty acres have transformed into true woodland.

Out of the 10,000 trees we planted I would guess 8000 have survived. The weaker ones are bleached and falling, but most are vigorous and strong.

We inspected the oak grove that had been previously suffering from an infection where the leaves were turning brown and curling, their surface covered in mildew.

It looked as though the rains had washed off the mildew, and we were happy to see that the oaks were offering new leaves. As Nietzsche would say, 'What does not kill me makes me stronger.' I hope that applies to oak trees as much as it does to foolish philosophers.

I was happy to see how well the willows were doing, because they generally do not like our acidic soil. My childhood, spent on the Thames, has left me with an affection for the willow, as has my seven children's favourite book, *The Wind in the Willows*. Of course, in the book the wildwood is the enemy, where the stoats and the weasels live, whereas the woods we are encouraging are benign.

I was so gratified that the saplings we planted thirty years ago are now mature trees. I thank Lee for pushing me over the forty acres of rough ground in my wheelchair.

I have marked the summer solstice for many years. It is well to remind ourselves that we are racing round the sun at 30 km per second and tipping towards it at the moment. When I was being taught this at school, it seemed so precarious and preposterous that I expected the teacher to say, 'Only kidding. You are on solid ground and it does not move.'

We used to have dinners for a few neighbours in the conservatory where we could watch the sky darkening above, the last light fading in the northwest and the first light rising in the northeast. When it got dark we lit the bonfire to encourage the sun to come back. One year Paolo Tullio's son Rocco got up from his seat and jumped through the fire. It became a ritual and in subsequent years we all had to do it. My next-door neighbour, Paddy Moloney of the Chieftains, would whip out his tin whistle to serenade the sun and help it to return. Paolo would sing Italian songs on his guitar that were both authentic and parody.

Each year the numbers increased until we reached the most we could seat at thirty-two. Famous people were aggrieved at not being invited. We decided to have one last blast. My then wife, Isabella, organized it. A marquee was required, and a band – and if you have a band people want to dance, so we needed a dance floor. We would have a big bonfire, of course, to drive the darkness away, but wouldn't fireworks be fun? Mick Jagger, an old friend, was invited. There was no room for celebs. Then one of the guards, hired to rebuff gatecrashers, reported that two men claiming to be Jack Nicholson and Michael Douglas wanted to get in. The party's reputation soared when people heard that Jack Nicholson and Michael Douglas really had crashed it.

At a certain point we invited guests to cross the river by stepping stones, where further revels were planned at Paolo's place. He had recently built a stone circle with large boulders he had acquired. They were aligned to the summer and winter solstices and the compass points. He claimed it was the first stone circle to be built in Ireland for 6000 years. There was another fire to jump through and his pond to jump into fully clothed or without clothes. Guests went round and round inside the stone circle, hoping for revelation.

This was the last party, but what a party it was.

I became a lapsed pagan.

Just as well we didn't have a party this year – it was cold and cloudy and probably rained. Keep your distance, please.

Rain. A grey cold day

I stood at the window watching the rain but it never stopped. It was that very wet rain that penetrates every surface and has the trees dripping and offering no shelter. My mind was as dull as the weather.

The dull wet weather of yesterday has carried over

The woods across the river have the exuberance of youth and our spirits soared to be among them. Now I am back with all my centurions: the eight-stemmed sycamore, the redwoods, the limes, the monkey puzzle, the Scots pines, the hawthorns, the aspens, the hazels, the Great Oak, the mighty larch, the long line of ancient oaks high on the slope and finally the twin oak, leaning over the river. These are the appropriate companions for an old man.

I salute them as I walk among them. For a stolen moment the sky is brighter and the air is warmer, but an angry, leaden cloud is heading this way. I feel the warmth of summer seeping up from the wet soil. The moss that crawls up the back of the twin oak is cold and sodden. I struggle to find some bark on which to signal. Below, the river surges for the sea and is in no mood for loitering. The low branches of the twin oak under the high river vibrate from the flow. Bird and squirrel, leaf and flow, rabbit and badger, man and bench, all under the twin oak's sphere of influence.

I hurry home. The black cloud pursues me.

24 JUNE

Sun woke me up at 6 am

Not a breath of wind, not a leaf stirring. Even the aspen leaf is hanging limp. Only the sun moves across its wide midsummer arc.

The birds are silent too. I go out quietly, respecting the silence and whomsoever cast this spell. The twin oak is tender. The rabbits leave reluctantly as I arrive. Only the river moves, but quietly, not even a gurgle.

As the outside world wakes up with a clatter, and traffic and planes resume, this feels like an end to silence, to peace.

During my career as a film-maker I often used silence to create tension or peace. Sound technicians frequently complained and urged me to put something on the soundtrack, at least an atmosphere. Silence was their foe, but it is my ally. Urban friends who stay in my house often complain of the silence, that it keeps them awake. Silence can remind us that we are falling through the void. Quick – turn up the music.

Sun, heat, windless

When I looked up from the myopia of my writing, I found myself in an empty house. I called out but my voice bounced back, muffled and muted.

Outside, it was as still as yesterday. Nothing moved. It reminded me of a recurring dream I had of dying and finding myself in a replica of my home and land.

I walked down among the lifeless leaves. Was I looking at a clever three-dimensional digital photograph? Was the afterlife digital reality?

Then I came upon the fallen oak. Every fungus and mushroom was feeding on it. It was cradled in long grass and a bouquet of foxgloves was growing out of its head. I was in the presence of death, so I knew I was alive.

My eye caught the movement of the river, the mystery of flow. The river had been running night and day for thousands of years, ever since the glacier melted.

I was alive, for a little while longer.

Hot, heavy, overcast

I woke up last night and threw off the covers. It was hot and airless. I opened the windows and gulped the heavy air.

In the distance, thunder rumbled. Flashes of lightning lit up the horizon. It did not stop. It grumbled closer. I counted the miles between flash and thunder: eight – five – three. I began to worry about the trees.

Half asleep, my mother was hustling us into the air-raid shelter, or if it was very cold, to huddle under the stairs. We boys could identify every plane, German or English, by the throb, whine, pulse of its engine, also the deep hum of a squadron. Most of all we rejoiced in the Rolls-Royce Merlin engine roar of the Spitfire.

The anti-aircraft guns would open up with a *crunch* and a *crunch* and a *crunch*. They did most of the damage as their exploded fragments rained down on our roofs.

We all had shrapnel collections. We would scour the streets after an air raid and sometimes the fragments were still hot. The dark, oily shrapnel of the incendiary bomb was greatly prized, as was the occasional detonator.

The violent storm was overhead. I feared for my trees. Let it hit the redwoods, their leaves can earth lightning. Thunder exploded violently. The bomb exploded across the street. The blast ripped all the glass out of our bay window even though it was criss-crossed with sticky paper. My mother, my sister and I were standing at the back of the room. Glass fragments came towards us in slow-motion silence. The blast had deafened us. Fear stretched time.

The blast reversed and sucked all the glass splinters away from our faces. We reproduced that scene in *Hope and Glory*. My SPFX man built a bellows with the same volume of air as the room. They put sugar glass into the windows. He placed a dynamite charge to force the bellows to expel the air and a second charge to immediately retract the air. As a film director you are allowed to put your nightmares on the screen, as well as your dreams.

Sleep came at last. This morning was fresh and clean, but rain was forecast. I searched for damage to the trees, I looked for burn marks on the redwood leaves but found none. Nevertheless, I like to think that the redwood saved the other trees.

Rain

One of my carers, Thérèse, is also a beekeeper, and I have invited her to put two hives into the walled garden to collect the lime-blossom honey. She just called to say it was too wet this morning. Try tomorrow. Luckily, the limes have not yet come to flower.

I venture out. Light rain is falling. Lee and his dog turn up. We agree how much we like the feel of this kind of rain on our faces. We walk together down to the gate. Beyond the gate is a passage of wild woods that we have not yet cultivated. It leads us to the public road. To our dismay, we find it covered with litter; cardboard cups and half-eaten sandwiches. There is so much of it that it feels like a deliberately aggressive act. Reluctantly, we decide that we must put a gate up at the public road. I will make an arrangement with the canoeists that they can have access, as they like to enter the river from here.

The other day a car was parked down there. The gardaí told us it belonged to a missing man who was suicidal. They found drugs in the car, and much later the missing man in the deep pond of a fish farm nearby. Everything leaves a shadow: the litter, the despairing man, the virus.

Wet and windy

I imagine it will be too wet today to transport the bees. We shall see. Then a message from Thérèse: she is bringing the bees despite the weather.

There is a mite that tries to get in the hives for the honey but is repelled by the guard bees. The mites then organize themselves into the shape of a bee and gain entry. This would suggest an intelligence not often found in a small insect. Bees, unlike mites, organize themselves to perform different functions for the common good.

The weather was worse, if anything. Violent gusts of wind and swirling rain, but Thérèse found a sheltered spot for the hive and the bees wait for the flowering of the limes.

What little I know of bees I learnt from Danny Rochford. He was the great beekeeper of Annamoe. He always brought us down a jar of clear lime-blossom honey to thank us for the trees. Danny never wore protection, even to his face, and I often saw his bare arms covered in bees, but they never stung him.

The bees arrived in the nick of time

I heard the drone from 50 yards away. When I got down into the middle of the cluster of the four limes that straddle our driveway, the drone had become a roar. I stood and gasped at its intensity, then I called Lili and Lee and they ran down to join me. The three of us, with our heads craning upwards, grinning at the joyful wonder of it, the power of it. We three had spent three months isolating together and here we were, holding hands and laughing.

LIME TREES

We have a cluster of lime trees here,
A guard of honour up to the house.
Unter den Linden, you might say.

Modestly,
the limes clothe their trunks with leaves,
making noble green oblongs of harmonious height.
In June they burst into improbable bloom,
hives erupt,
and the roaring bees follow greedily on,
feasting on those delicate white flowers.
Lime pollen is mildly narcotic to bees,
They often fall drunkenly out of the tree.

The last day of the month and my final entry in this journal

This lockdown must have been hard if you lived on the tenth floor of a tower block with two small children under your feet, but we had a large house and land to wander in and a river to swim in. My lack of mobility had already locked me down to this place. My son, Lee, and my daughter, Lili Mae, had isolated with me. It was a privilege and a joy to have them back in the house.

When we were first locked down, I decided I would see all my favourite films. In fact, I didn't screen a single film during lockdown. We soon stopped watching the TV news. We checked the facts on our phones. We gradually discarded all the distractions that chop up our days, including our phones. Distractions from what? From the attempt to understand the nature of which we are a part.

The overarching insight that I intuited from my connections to the trees is that our subconscious (which we learn is making many of our decisions) is closely linked to the force that tells trees when to leaf, birds to migrate, us to fall in love.

We must modestly allow ourselves to be led. I am not the 'captain of my soul', I am a poor creature trying to connect.

CYCLICAL

Lee Boorman

During the lockdown, in the spring and early summer of 2020, I was fortunate to be working remotely in my childhood home in Annamoe, Co. Wicklow, self-isolating with my father and younger sister.

The house is an old rectory that Dad bought fifty years ago, surrounded by woodland, meadows and streams. It – or more specifically, the land – is the host of my fondest childhood memories and is to this day the site of many of my escapist daydreams (especially now that I have returned to Dublin).

I spent the majority of the days hunched over my computer or on the phone, responding to the various queries or projects directed to me. However, early in the morning before work began, or late in the evening when it had abated, the lockdown also enabled me to explore the land where I grew up, to an extent that I have not been able to do since I left the Glebe at nine years of age.

I climbed trees that I had not climbed in fifteen years. I swam daily (or as close to daily as possible) in rivers and lakes in the Wicklow mountains. I caught trout, snared rabbits and watched birds.

I have been in stare-offs with the deer that graze these hills. I have been allowed to witness a miniscule fraction of the life of the elusive kingfisher, spirit of the river. The heron has watched me with its haughty contempt, and the red squirrel has fled from me (unwarrantedly, of course, though he could not know that I would not harm him).

I also toured the land with my father, who has lived in and loved this place for half a century. We spoke of trees, of the river, and the wildlife that were our neighbours. He shared his experiences, his regrets, and, remarkably after all this time, his remaining hopes for the land.

I was given the pleasure of witnessing the true power of the place through him as we rambled together during this time.

One warm day we decided that we would swim in the river that runs through the land, the Avonmore. We used to swim here regularly, and this activity was a favourite of Dad's and mine. However, it had been beyond his reach since he lost the strength in his legs.

Nevertheless, together we were able to make our way down to an area where the river runs deep. A place where he taught me (and my six other siblings) to swim.

I managed to shift, push and pull him off the bank and into the water. For a moment we stood there, hesitant, inching forward, him gripping my arm as we slowly made our way towards the centre of the river.

But once Dad was waist-deep, magic happened. In the river he stood without my aid, supported only by his arms paddling in the water and by the gentle embrace of the current. All hesitation drifted away and he plunged in with abandon, enveloped by the black waters. I waited with no small amount of trepidation for him to resurface. After a moment-long eternity he did, and I swam alongside him, giving gentle guidance or direction when needed.

After a few minutes of swimming, the river gave another gift: it returned to Dad his confidence; confidence enough to disregard the flotation device provided to him by a well-meaning but paternalistic doctor. Then, after fully submitting to the river, Dad gained a boyishness, an excitement, a desire to splash and dive and play.

He smiled and laughed; perhaps he even shed a discreet tear? But that is between him and the river.

Regardless of the weather, the Avonmore retains a frigidly cold core, making it almost a penance to swim in. When I was twelve, Dad took me to the Midnight Sun Film Festival in Finland. During that trip we were brought to a true glacial lake, deep in the Arctic Circle. We alternated between hot saunas and dips in the ice water. Thanks in no small part to the many years we spent swimming in the Avonmore, which has its own glacial past, Dad and I did not shame ourselves amongst the chionophilic Finns.

However, Dad feels the cold more these days, and I admit I was feeling less than warm at this point myself. So I asked if he wanted to get out.

'Can we go across to the stone once more?' was his reply.

How could I refuse such a reasonable request? The river had given him back the years that he had spent, if only for the length of our swim.

On another day during our joint isolation, we decided to venture into the groves of native woodland that Dad had planted almost thirty years previously. I roamed those woods often, mostly following my dog as she explored the various scents and trails. However, Dad had not returned to be amongst his trees for years due to his poor mobility.

The groves lie in a glen nestled between three hills and two rivers. They were planted in an naturalistic, asymmetric way to mimic the flow of a stream, or the meandering of deer trails, making them a leafy paradise for a wild young boy.

But what was once human-designed woodland (even so as to resemble a natural forest) had been reclaimed entirely. Birds, rabbits and deer were its residents and their signs were abundant. The trees themselves, which had grown out as well as up, had knocked over the fences put in place to protect them from ravenous herbivores, and in this way they had accentuated the natural form of the groves. Most inspiring of all, saplings had sprung up in the corridors of grassland between the trees – notwithstanding the derelict fencing – thereby doing away with the last remnants of man's influence.

It had become a true young wildwood.

When I was a boy, Dad and I would walk in these woods together. He would send me into a grove and wait on the other side for me to navigate my way through the thick underbrush. He would then ask me to name the trees I had seen along the way.

Oak, ash, alder, birch, willow, aspen, beech, holly, lime, pine, larch.

I learnt them all; not only their names, but the shape of their leaf, the texture of their bark, how tall they grew, how wide, when they came into leaf and when they gave them up in the autumn. I came to love them not just for how high I could climb or how they would allow me to hide from the outside world, but for their features, for their diversity and for their warmth.

Now, as I pushed Dad's wheelchair across the long tufts of bog grass and under the branches (making this woodland wheelchair-accessible, I might add), he would point out a tree and ask me its name – not to test me, but hoping that my young eyes could compensate for his old ones. My childhood training had paid off, however, as Dad's face would light up upon hearing the name of the trees, his memory stirring:

'Ah yes, a pedunculate oak – it has that tail on the leaf. We planted mostly sessile oaks because the woods along Loch Dan and Glendalough are sessile. But I have a fondness for the pedunculate oak, so, I planted a few of those as well.'

When we approached the largest grove, full of oak and birch and aspen, I offered to carry Dad on my back as we had reached the wheelchair's limit. I hoisted him up and took a hesitant step forward. His weight was not insurmountable, but a grown man is an awkward thing to carry. The ambience of the woods, and Dad's weight on my back, jolted back memories: Dad had carried me on his shoulders for years ('uppity', we called it) and through this very woodland, though at that time both the trees and I were much smaller.

Now, as I held Dad and he gazed in wonder at the unending green, any strain I felt by his weight was alleviated. We walked into the heart of our small forest and marvelled at its growth. In his lifetime he had planted these trees as saplings, cared for them, and now he got to witness their adolescence. They will outlive him, and me, but we were granted a premonition of the great woodland that they will one day become.